Poems and Stori-yarns

A collection of writings spanning the years
1937 to 2008

by Betty Willis

BETTY WILLIS

ISBN 978-0-9923037-2-3

General photographs Betty Willis
Drawings and graphic layout by Dana McCown
Front Cover photograph by Betty Willis
Back cover photograph by Douglas Head
Copyright ©2009 Betty Willis

StoryBridge Press

Table of contents

Poems Introduction v

Early Poems 1

Silhouetted Things 1
Twilight Reverie 2
The Captive Cockatoo 4
Memory's Treasury 6
The Church That David Loved 8
Gold 10
Sight To The Blind 12
Moonlight 14
Faith 15
They Grew in Silence 16
Alexandra House, Easter 1947 17
Here Lies Mystery 18
The Craftsman's Hand 20
St Stephen's Anniversary 100 Years 22

A Little Nonsense 24

A Little Nonsense Now And Then 24
Dedicated To Josephine 24
A Queer Idea 26
Give It A Title And You Can Have It 27
The Procrastinator 27
Aussie Vegemites 28

Australian Poems 29

The Forest 29
Autumn Evening 29
The Bunya Mountains 30

On The Overnight Bus To Sydney	31
The Storm	32
Weather Report	33

The Pacific   34

Return To Papua New Guinea	34
Rabaul Market	36
To Toowoomba With Love On An Autumn Day	38
To Toowoomba In September From Tinghi, S.I.	40
Eratap	42
The Coconut – A Woman's Vision	44
The Pandanus Basket	47
To The People Of Epi	49
How Can You Be Sure	50

Stori-Yarns Introduction   51

Get It Off	52
Washing Day	53
Of Books And Reading	55
The Best Thing Since Sliced Bread	57
Keep A Thing – Its Use Will Come	59
Ham And Eggs	61
What's That You Said?	62
Solomon Islands – Guadalcanal-Seghe	65
Of Ablutions And Sundry Related Matters	67
On The Plane - Vanuatu	71
No Chance Of A Postcard	72
Yupela Laik Save Tok Pidgin?	74
What Am I Here After?	77
Old Age Isn't For Sissies	79

Introduction

Poetry

This little book illustrates the growth of thinking and versifying of a young girl in an isolated situation in the Australian bush, onward to day by day situations in various settings and to cherished experiences amongst friends around the Pacific.

Many of the early poems had their origins as this girl sat on the western steps of a country home, towel and soap in hand, waiting her turn in the shower under the high tank outside, as the late afternoon faded into dusk. In the background was at first the knowledge and fear that the world was sliding into war, and then the actuality of the years of conflict.

Later poems take a leap from the sixties to the eighties. What happened to those years? As far as writing goes, they seem to have been filled with business letters, minutes, reports, submissions - **and** eight years in Papua New Guinea. Then creativity resurfaced with reflections on Australian surroundings and vivid memories of episodes in the beloved Pacific, culminating in the demanding but rewarding venture of writing and publishing my memoirs. Some of these poems were included in the memoirs but most are seeing the light of day for the first time.

Photo Betty Willis

Early Poems
Silhouetted Things

Tall flowers against a window,
Tall trees against the sky,
What do they hold of beauty
To haunt the seeing eye?

A hill-top church uprear'ed
Against a cloud-draped moon,
Majestic, arching bridges
In summer's brittle noon;

Fine tracery of branches
At even's etching time,
Each slender limb a poem,
Each fragile twig a rhyme;

To me there is a beauty
In silhouetted things
To clutch with urgent fingers
The aching heart-strings.

1946

Twilight Reverie

As dusk on tiptoe gently steals
Across the whisp'ring land,
All Nature holds her breath in awe
Awaiting Night's soft hand.

I pause with silent Nature too,
Awaiting Night's decree,
And thoughts of all Eternity
Softly come to me.

Sometimes I ask what use it is
To strive for good – in vain –
Why seek to make earth nearer heav'n
If war still comes again?

What use is it to make a home
With garden set around,
To build it slowly day by day
When war might all confound?

But, softly through the twilight dim
A voice comes silently,
"O mortal, cease thy worrying
And trust thine all with Me.

"I made the world thou dwellest in,
   Man did I fashion, too,
So think'st thou not that I can guide
   And right the wrong men do?

From evil I can bring forth good,
   And right must conquer wrong;
So, mortal, cease from worrying –
   Have faith, for I am strong."

So words I gleaned in the gath'ring dusk
   Gave faith in the fate of earth,
Knowing it lies not in human hands
   Nor depends on human worth.
            1939

The Captive Cockatoo

Poor cag'ed bird! Alone you sit,
Your listless wings hang loose,
Your drooping head and ragged tail –
Do they bespeak abuse?
Or is it just that life is vain
If freedom cannot come again?

They cramp you in a tiny cage,
Whose boast for years has been
That all within their land are free –
Your plight they have not seen:
And yet the freedom you did own
Was wider far than they have known.

You once soared up on tireless wings
With scrub stretched far below,
One lonely speck in azure blue.
What joy it was to know
Yours was the freedom of the skies,
Untrammelled liberty your prize!

Or else you flew in company strong
Whose harsh notes rent the air,
And lighting on some kingly tree,

You stripped till all was bare,
And left the gaunt limbs raised on high,
Your wanton ruin to decry.

Then rose the flock one cloud of white
Which caught the sun's bright rays,
So dazzling in its purity
It hurt the eyes to gaze:
And sweeping on beyond the trees,
Left but a cry, borne on the breeze.

Left but a cry – and now you raise
Your head and give your call.
Only an echo mocks your voice:
Your prison cage's wall
Forbids all hope of liberty
And naught but death can set you free.

1939

Memory's Treasury

Thanks be for peace that will not fade
While memory can recall
The scent of flowers at eventide
On whispering breezes wafted wide.
An incense sweet enfolding all.

Thanks be for lawns of emerald green
Dappled with light and shade
Shades that are trembled endlessly
With peeking rays that strive to see
The flickering patterns ere they fade.

For gum-trees reaching heavenward:
Slim trunks of virgin white
Clear-cut against a cloudless sky,
And green heads proudly held on high
Proclaiming wide their kingly right.

Or stark limbs bared to a changing sky
Grey with the coming night.
The ceaseless hum of insects small
The slow descent of even's pall
The last swift fading of the light.

For the breathless hush of a summer noon
With slumber quieted:
For the mystic spell of a moon-drenched night
That draws to the orb of its silent light
The glory of ages long since dead.

Thanks be for beauties gathered in
To memory's treasury.
Mid stress of life I'll steal aside,
Open the gates of memory wide
And these shall soothe my soul for me.
1940

The Church That David Loved

How lovely are Thy dwelling places, Lord,
Thy sweet voiced psalmist, David, knew of old.
He heard amid the incense drifting high,
Amid the chanting of a thousand tongues,
That sped their gladdening praise above, a Voice
That said "Be still and know that I am God."

And, through the years of fleeting change, the years
Of lessons learnt in suffering and pain,
Learnt but to be forgotten once again
In that fierce race and struggle men call life,
That voice has come,
So that the lessons were not wholly lost,
Although the way seemed dark, and faint, and slow.
And shining through the mists of Time, the church
That David loved has called the weary home.

So still the Church enfolds who'er will come –
Blessed are they who can. Within its walls
The organ notes roll solemnly and slow,
And grandly swell and rise in glorious dreams,
Then gently fall to trembling hopes and joys,
Bearing aloft on waves of melody
Prayers for the future, brave and fair with hope:

And people's voices rise in glad accord
With praise and thanks to that Great God of Love,
While in the silence fraught with sanctity
Tired heads and hearts bow down and seek for peace,
And hearts grow lighter as they hear her wings.

'Neath their soft beat all earthly troubles flee;
How needless seem our fretting and our strife,
How paltry are the worldly bickerings
Against the background of Eternity!
So silence, "eld'st of things," falls like a balm
On lonely heart and troubled soul and mind
And, crowning all, the quiet Benediction
To carry strength throughout the waiting days.

1941

Gold

There is the gold the miser hoards –
A fascinating stream
Flowing between his bony hands
Like quivering precious strings of sands
That light, yet curse, his every dream.

Gold of adventurous buccaneers
Treasured in tales of old;
Cursed with the blood of countless men,
Piled high in the pirates' secret den,
Magnetic, costly, fateful gold.

But there is gold I hold more dear
Than all your pirates' hoard.
It bears no tale of strife and crime,
No history in every clime
Of war and struggle, fire and sword –

Gold in the garden gleaming bright,
Vital and fresh and free:
Nasturtium gold mid leaves of green,
Shy gold violas scarcely seen,
Bright poppies flaunting for the bee;

Soft sunlight seeping through the trees,
Soaking the woods with heat;
Such drowsy, dreaming, golden days –
'Neath sleepy veil of sunlit haze
I almost hear the earth's heart beat.

Crisp nights of crystal clarity,
Clear heavens spangled gold,
Soft radiance o'er earth and sky
Cleft by the mournful curlew's cry –
What cherished dreams does wise Moon hold?

Welcoming gold of the homestead lights,
Clear-cut through darkest night,
Proclaiming tidings of light and cheer,
Of comfort though the night be drear,
Of shelter, friendliness and light;

Flames in the fireplace leaping high,
Unchecked and undismayed,
Symbol of leaping, golden dreams
That light our path with beck'ning gleams
And bid us strive for what we prayed.

1941

Sight to The Blind

The scales have fallen from my eyes;
Where I was blind I now can see;
In all the maze and whirl of thing
Is centre of tranquillity.

Where once confusion dimly reigned
Are meaning, law and order, peace,
For now at last one word of Thine
Has bade the old disorder cease.

"I am the Truth," You said, "the Light,"
And all so suddenly I saw
That Truth were Truth indeed, if it
Applied from low to highest law.

If all the things You daily marked
Are governed by a rule Divine –
If seed springs up in fertile ground;
If branch bears only through the vine;

If shepherd caring for his flock
Is but obeying Love's high call;
If fatherhood's forgiveness free
Reflects the Father of us all –

If all the things that I can know
Have meaning in eternal sight,
Through them I reach to things unseen,
And lo! the Sun breaks through the Night.

Then Morn's horizons widen out,
No cloud can blot – through blue and grey
Eyes that have glimpsed eternal Truth
Look onward to eternal Day.

1944

Moonlight

Among the trees the moonlight gently stole,
The trunks stood black against the growing light,
Deep murky pools of darkness baffled sight
While quiet ranged around each tall tree's bole,
And peace that crept into my very soul.
The glory of the moon that lit the night
So great it was I thought that naught could blight
The joy it gave to hearts from pole to pole.

A lacy pattern twining branches wove
Of dark against the moon's cold, silent beams –
A pattern flecked with pale moon's silver gleams.
The trees stirred gently 'neath the breeze's sigh,
The moon smiled down benignly from above,
And Peace and Quiet with folded wings drew nigh.

1938

Faith

Faith is a star that mounts the skies
Untrammelled, unconfined,
While Reason climbs with laboured steps
The ladder of thought behind.

Faith is the lamp that lights the way
When growing shadows foil.
And Reason fires his torch from Faith
And bends anew to toil.

Faith is the power to lift a man
From mere earthbound control.
Reason must walk the roads with him
But Faith gives wings to his soul.

Faith is the beam to hold him true
To the ultimate good and goal;
Through skyways vast it leads him home
To One Who planned the whole.

1945

They Grew in Silence

Obscurity in shadowed garb has walked in many lives:
In silence cloaked, how many great have seen the slow years roll,
In what deep ways has time achieved maturing of a soul?

Did David, under arching skies, in quiet before his God,
Seek out infinity of thought and touch the Eternal Mind,
And learn to walk as friend of God, to find Him wondrous kind?

And Christ, Who lived so many years for such brief ministry –
I wonder in what ways He strove throughout His silent youth,
To forge with each day's common round another link of truth.

Oh Lord, may we with patience tread the pathway set before,
Content, although we cannot see the motives of Thy heart,
Convinced that in the Eternal Scheme we have our destined part.

1947

Alexandra House, Easter 1947

Oh Lord, we render thanks to Thee
For friendship's flowers blooming
In this glad spot beside the sea.
Their fragrance long shall cherished be
When we once more have parted.

Thy peace, O Christ, we've touched on here;
We've seen Thy Spirit shining
In faces now to us grown dear
As we have seen them year by year
In service freely rendered.

We'll carry through the mundane days
The mem'ry of the union
Of heart and voice in joyful praise,
And through our work once more we'll raise
The theme songs of our gladness.

1947

Here Lies Mystery

Lo, here lies mystery; not in the strange
Dramatic happenings in man's domain,
But in the quiet awakening of buds to spring;
The swelling green on myriad boughs,
The silent call that quickens all these things.
What greater mystery can we see than life
Burst gladly forth from some small wizened seed?

How could the golden glow of marigolds
Have lain imprisoned in that dry, brown husk?
A darkened pod could never hold
The strength and vigour, grace and majesty
That are enshrine´d in a stately tree –
And yet, it does!

"Except a corn of wheat fall into the ground
And die, it abideth alone; but if it die
It bringeth forth much fruit."
Ah, this is mystery indeed; here dwells
The mystery of all the universe,
And we stand awed before it.

What cannot be, if this be so?
And through the limits of our human minds

We can envisage greater thing ahead,
When, bursting from the confines of this life,
Knowledge and feeling and the power to do
May blossom forth to all eternity.
1948

The Craftsman's Hand

A little bit of beauty
That we have made our own;
A garden gay with colour
From seeds our hands have sown;

A picture truly painted;
A garment deftly wrought
Or words in flowing rhythm
Each shade of meaning caught;

And we, O God Creator,
Stretch out a craftsman's hand
To touch for a brief moment
The Master Artisan.

The beauty we have captured
Has brought us nearer Thee:
Thou hast a universe to build,
And, toiling humbly, we

Have made such little fragments,
But through our tiny part
We've come to comprehend the love
Of beauty in Thy heart.

And when we hear of loveliness
That seldom meets man's sight –
The majesty of Arctic lands,
Pure snowdrifts, dazzling white,

Of sunsets on a thousand hills,
Scenes of the ocean deep,
Or hidden in the bushland
Wildflowers that shyly peep –

We'll never say, "What pity
Such beauty goes to waste,"
But feel it is Thy sanctuary,
And with Thy Presence graced.

Thou, too, must have Thy quiet spots
To meditate alone
To glory in the beauty of
The things Thy Hands have sown
1949

St Stephen's Anniversary 100 Years

O God, who art our Father great;
From Thy hands are our blessings sent.
Accept the thanks we offer now
For all the passing years have meant.

For times of patient labouring,
For service quiet and unseen;
For courage in the little things;
For all our heritage can mean.

For those who built in brick and stone
A church to grace a city fair;
For those who built in human hearts
With love and faith and patient care.

And now, oh Lord, we pray Thee more
To send us forth with blessings new –
With insight fill our hearts afresh,
With courage strong our steps endue.

Show us the need of those who dwell
In harder and in hungrier lands;
Show us the need of neighbours near;
Teach us to see the outstretched hands.

Live in us, Servant Lord of all,
That young and old alike may know,
The moving of Thy Spirit sure,
The guidance of Thy will below.
1963

A Little Nonsense
A Little Nonsense Now and Then

"A little nonsense now and then
Is relished by the wisest men"
And of course by women, too,
But for them the rhymes are few.
1998

Dedicated To Josephine

Do not call me "lady," please –
Shades of "the lady wife!"
I don't like "luv" or "dear" or "ducks,"
"Cheese and kisses" or "trouble and strife."

"Woman" is a good strong word,
But hopeless for the poet.
For, try to find a rhyme for it,
And you will surely blow it.

And "Missus" is so ugly, sure,
And "Ms" is even worse,
And if you call a "Mrs." – "Miss"
She can get very terse.

"Mr." has a solid sound
And "Master" speaks of power.
Match it up with "Mistress" though,
And see the glances lower.

"Bloke's" a good Australian word,
Or "Mate" – just take your pick,
But call a woman "Sheila"
And it reeks of Ginger Mick.

Here's a resolution then
In our vocabu-lary –
In speaking of the female kind
Please be very wary.

1998

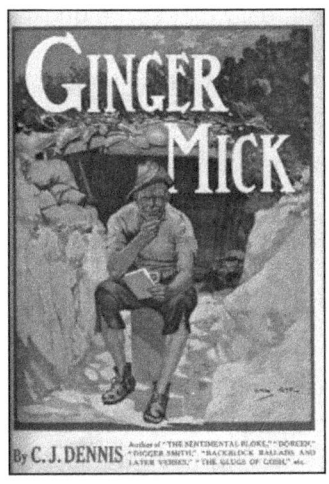

A Queer Idea
(as a boarder at Fairholme College in 1937)

As I stood on my head in the bath tub
A queer thought came to me.
If all the girls were like centipedes
How funny that would be.

Oh, just imagine if you dare to
Each with a hundred feet,
Oh, wouldn't they form a relay team
Dreadfully hard to beat?

Just to think of the clatter they'd make
Galloping down the stairs
Is enough to make one white in the face
And rob one of one's hairs.

When I think of all the shoes to clean
It really makes me quake,
And imagination of the shoe bags
Keeps me at night awake.

And all the stockings there'd be to darn
Would fill me with despair.
Just wouldn't they fill the clothes line up
A-waving in the air?

When I think of them marching all in "croc,"
The tramp their feet would make,
I'm glad they aren't really centipedes
Or else my heart would break.
1937

Give It a Title and You Can Have It

The sporgy screws are loud to lose.
Alas alas too far the views.
Anent the skies the skerrick runs;
The rounded wombok scans the clouds;
Too far and deep and dense the shrouds.

Oh me, oh my, the bonks are dumb,
The slithered skoons all skungy come.
Afar the gadzooks haunt the hills.
The boinky bhlathers baulk the bills.
Beneath the callumpathic skies
Omnoscious incombent lies.
1985

The Procrastinator

Jacaranda blooms are fading,
Christmas bush is reddening,
Hydrangeas and agapanthus have bloomed
To grace school speech days.
The postie arrives later each day
Leaving an offering of cards and newsletters
Produced by ever-advancing technology.

But my humble computer waits in vain
For the forty-seventh edition of "Betty's Budget."
Tomorrow I'll get started!
2008

Aussie Vegemites

We're happy little Vegemites,
Our arteries stuffed with salt,
And if our blood chlorest'rol's high
it's really not our fault.

We love to eat our pizza meals,
We dote on take-aways;
Potato flakes and chips and crimps
Enliven all our days.

And as for what can quench our thirst
It comes in cans or bottles
Of coke and fizz, of wine and beer -
No **water** wets our throttles.

We take our tea with sugarine -
We have to watch our weight,
But leave the icecream there to help
Our calcium intake.

Yes, we're health-conscious Aussie types,
We try to get it right
But are we "Life be in it" fans
Or Norms who only might?
1981

Australian Poems
The Forest

I walked a forest track today.
Beneath my feet the dead leaves lay;
Smooth-trunked the gum trees towered tall
And quiet muffled each footfall.

The soft light greenly filtered through;
No insect called, no small bird flew.
Through twisting vine and stately palm
No whisper stirred cathedral calm.

1993

Autumn Evening

A lone currawong calls ku-wah, ku-wahhh.
Bleak breezes curl around the corners;
The sun's long shafts lie across the land
And Autumn's warning sends a shiver down my spine.

In long-practised answer
I draw the curtains, turn on the lights –
And in the snugness of familiar room
The grey ghost of loneliness retreats once more.

1994

The Bunya Mountains

Wind in the trees and the currawongs calling,
Rainforests dripping and gentle streams falling,
Chortle of jackasses, black crows a-quarking,
Whip birds a-cracking and cat birds a-barking.

Midnight blue bowerbirds, green patterned rosellas,
Fairy wrens flitting neath thorny umbrellas,
Yellow breast robins that hop and that twitter,
Bush turkeys busily scratching the litter.

The peace of the mountains is here to enfold us.
The magic of mountains continues to hold us;
Evening creeps on and draws out the sun's rays
And under the bunyas a wallaby plays.

1985

On The Overnight Bus to Sydney

Today I saw the full moon
Farewell retreating night
Sinking in a glowing ball
Below the hills from sight.

Then I saw the day creep
Across the land below,
The hills like paper cut-outs
Against the morning glow.

My heart leapt up to see it,
A silent leap of praise,
For this one golden moment
Will linger all my days.

1995

The Storm

The air hangs heavy with warning
Of violence to come;
The birds perch motionless waiting,
Ready to flee for home;
The wind in the branches rallies
Its forces ready to strike.
The piled clouds gather in silence
Waiting the thunder's drum.

Autumn leaves gold and russet
Dance to the wind's swift beat,
Stinging, the rain drops patter
Meeting the earth's trapped heat.
Up from the asphalt rises
A swirling mist of steam;
Lightning strikes at one with thunder
Then, pouring, bursting – RAIN.

1995

Weather Report

"Showers today but passing through,
Tomorrow's skies clear and blue.
Weekend fine, good for sport.
Enjoy yourselves! This ends report."

*(Grass is withered, earth is cracked,
Cattle dying, crops are black.
Not a cloud, skies are clear,
Pitiless the sun shines here.)*

"A cyclone up Rockhampton way,
Moving seawards – we're OK.
Only winds and heavy rain;
Weekend will be bright again."

*(Coconuts are stripped and torn,
Many years to bear again.
Bananas pulped, while fish all hide,
People killed in mountainslide.)*

Give us, Lord, ears to hear
Voices crying loud and clear:
Not the claim of weekend sport
But human lives in each report.

1992

The Pacific
Return to Papua New Guinea

It is not always joyful, going back,
But my journey into yesterday was glad.
Maybe the trees are not as plentiful
(The enthusiastic axe or nature's winds to blame?)
Flamboyant hibiscus have missed the loving touch;
The buildings sag in spots and mould accrues –
But your greetings were as warm, your love as open,
Your tears of joy or sympathy as free to flow.
You have grown, matured, gladly grasped the torch
And pushed ahead in your own way –
Not ours perhaps, (but that we knew and hoped for).
What we brought you, seedling in a western pot,
Has taken root in your own soil, grown, borne fruit.
And tears of frustration I once wept
Were purged with your memories and anecdotes
Of fruit your lives have borne.

Some tales you told I could not recall,
But you had held them in your hearts across the years,
And as you told hold love and learnings then
Had helped you serve in villages and towns,

In face of mining giants
Or guns and scorched earth of rebel gangs,
My heart was filled with tears of thankfulness
That I had shared your growing life and faith.

It is not always joyful, going back,
But I – I have been blessed beyond all words.
1992.

Rabaul Market

Rabaul Market

Bus and truck and hapka,
Blare of motor horn,
Dropping off their cargo
As the day is born.

Baskets full of kaukau,
Singapore and yam,
Taro, cabbage, beans and corn,
Sauersop and rambutan;

Pineapple and pawpaw,
Yellow, red and gold.
Banana, mangos, butterfruit,
Kulau sweet and cold.

Turtle eggs and fresh-baked bread,
Tobacco laid in lines,
Pepper, lime and betel nut –
But watch for spitting fines!

Meri blouse and laplap,
Necklaces of seeds,
Deep-sea shells and snail shells,
Spider shells and beads;

Graceful curve of dolphin
Caught in polished wood,
Seahorses and dugong –
Tap the tourist mood.

Babel sounds of place talk,
Laughter, quarrels too,
Bare feet, thonged feet,
Here and there a shoe.

Black skins and brown skins,
Skins of every shade,
Sleepy baby, crying child -
How much kina have we made?

Pack the truck and head for home
Underneath the palms,
Scent of frangipani,
Crotons' brilliant arms.

Mother Mountain watches,
Vulcan slumbers yet,
And far across the harbour
Smoke grey the sun has set.

1992

To Toowoomba With Love On An Autumn Day

I could be playing bridge or crib
As many seniors do –
But I am crossing opal seas
In a dugout canoe.

I could be walking city streets
With shops and buildings tall –
But now I pass on dusty roads
Trade store and market stall.

I could be shivering in the cold
Or braced by mountain air –
But I am sweltering in the heat
With sticky face and hair,

Or fronting waves in powered canoe,
The salt spray on my lips,
While on the bay triumphant flags
Flutter on Taiyo ships.

I don't look out on springtime blooms,
Neat lawns and gardens planned –

Pandanus grow and crotons blaze,
Palms lean across the sand.

Instead of hearing Aussie speech
And following Aussie ways,
My ears and tongue are stretched to cope
With unfamiliar phrase.

I do not watch from easy chair
The TV news and "soaps."
Instead I sit on bamboo floors
While people share their hopes.
1992

To Toowoomba in September From Tinghi, Solomon Islands

Today your gardens proudly bloom,
The tourists come to gaze,
Across the streets the banners hang,
Below, the traffic maze.

Here, village life moves quiet and slow,
Thatched roofs drip last night's rain,
The smoke of fresh-lit cooking fires
Drifts skyward once again.

The children play, a baby cries,
The big red rooster crows,
With scrape of fresh-husked coconut
The pile of white flesh grows.

The river flows beneath the trees,
Sea beats on coral bays;
And if the sky is fine tonight
The men will dive for "crays."

Today they pull the big canoe
Down from the mountainside.

At last the work of axe and adze
Will meet the running tide;

And through the tired and aching limbs
That pulled with one accord
Their common work and common goal
Will find its rich reward.
1994

Eratap

The wind blows strong at Eratap,
The air moves cool and free
Through mango, palm and breadfruit leaves.
Below, the blue, clear sea.

The road drops down from Eratap,
The trucks jolt on their way
With people bound for work or school
Or food for market day.

But death has come to Eratap,
The village strangely still
As people make their silent way
Slowly down the hill.

For life's events at Eratap
Touch closely on each one.
No isolated grief is here –
This was our sister's son.

So flowers and food and flowing tears
Express a common grief
For this young man with promise filled
Whose life has been so brief.

Yes, death has come to Eratap
And I from far away
Have little left that I can share –
Their grief must have its day.

1995

The Coconut – A Woman's Vision

You came upon the swelling tide
Storm tossed, sunburnt, salt-soaked –
And then you reached the shore.
Tossed high, the sand embraced you,
The gentle rain now washed you,
Sun's warmth woke roots within you
That sought the nourishment beneath,
While, breaking forth above, the first green leaves
Reached up towards the sun.

Slow was the growth but sure.
Straight trunk proudly standing
At last bore fruit –
Fruit to meet so many needs –
For food and drink and flavour,
Leaves, too, that serve for shelter and so many skills;
And when the cyclones came, you bent but did not break.
Maybe your leaves were shredded, your fruit spoiled,
But you will stand, bear fruit again.

I too, a woman, came, tossed by many storms,
Confined by culture, held back by fear,
Pressed down by pre-conceived ideas,
Bent under many burdens.
But there came One who said, "woman, you are free"
And so in hope I stand.

The storms still come, but now
I bend before them but I do not break.
Sometimes the fruit of my efforts is scattered,
My leaves are shredded by criticism,
My growth is stunted by patriarchy,
But still I stand;
And when I see a coconut palm, my sister,
I take heart, take heart.

1996

BETTY WILLIS

The Pandanus Basket

Stripped and trimmed,
Boiled and sundried,
Cut into widths
Ready to weave.
I can stay as one,
A solitary strip,
Or I can offer myself
To be woven with other strips.

In and out, across and back,
Turning to make a shape,
Colours blending into a pattern,
Till at last we stand together,
No longer simply strips of pandanus
But a basket, ornamental, useful,
Ready for many purposes;
To be used, to serve,
To find fulfilment.

Will I stay quietly in my corner, isolated,
Or will I join my sisters
And find a wider purpose?

1996

BETTY WILLIS

To The People of Epi

We laughed and talked and learned together,
Shared food and customs.
"It's only our local food," you said
As you took us into your lives
And into your hearts,
Foreseeing our every need.

But a few short days and then we moved on –
Another village, new faces,
Experiences filtered through different personalities,
Another farewell, your love expressed in word and gift,
Then on again.

Now coral shores and blue, blue seas
Leaning palms and thatched houses,
Rock-roughened roads, sun, rain and wind,
Are just a memory.
So too the curious children, softly feeling white skins
Or gently fanning our sweat-drenched faces.

But a memory that warms the heart
And reaches back across the miles.

1996

How Can You Be Sure
Memories of working at Seghe

"How can you be sure
There are no rats behind the door,
Mice that squeak and gnaw,
White ants in the floor,
Borers in the bed – and more!
Spiders in the shower,
Cockroaches by the score,
Mossies that whine and bore,
Persistent ants galore??
You can't!"

I was inspired to burst into verse, with apologies
to a certain well-known pest exterminator –
1998

Stori-Yarns

Storytelling still lingers with us as a tradition that dates back to the pre-writing era, when stories were passed down from generation to generation - the centuries of oral history.

My story-telling and story-hearing experiences started with bush yarns told by men as they squatted in the dust of outback Queensland, or sat, legs stretched out, back against a tree as they ate their stale bread and cold mutton sandwiches and drank black tea out of a quart pot.

The next story-sharing memory that lingers is of Brisbane in wartime, with electricity blackouts, a group of boarding house friends sitting on the floor on eiderdowns, brewing tea over the flame of a little methylated spirit stove.

Cherished memories are "stori-yarns" shared with friends, seated on the floors of village houses around the Pacific – tales of "taim bilong tumbuna" (old times) or vividly recounted hilarious incidents or serious discussions of lives and beliefs.

In later years it has been the stimulation of a "Writers at Work" group as reading meetings have encouraged the sharing of a wide variety of original creations and memories which have brought forth urgings, "That's history. It should be recorded."

So here are some "stori-yarns" and memories.

Get It Off

"Get it off," I screamed as I raced, sobbing and terrified down the long verandah - but out of the corner of my eye I could see the black spider still following me. When the verandah ran out and my mother caught up with me, I found I was running away from a dead spider caught onto my dress by a length of web. "The time Betty was chased by a dead spider" was used as a taunt by my brothers for what seemed like years.

I must have been about four or five years old when this happened, and it was about the same time when I made another faux pas that haunted me for a long time. The topic of the royal family had come up in a discussion between visitors and my parents. One of the adults commented that Queen Victoria had been on the throne for 60 years. I can still hear myself, with visions of a regal figure seated on that throne all those years, saying in a small voice, "She must have got terribly tired" and I can feel my embarrassment at the barely concealed amusement of the adults.

But I am sure, seated on the throne or not, there must have been times when Queen Victoria felt like screaming - not "Get it off!" but "Get me off it!"

2002

Washing Day

The other day I got to thinking of WASHING DAY. It all started with boiled rice - but let me explain.

Washing day was always Monday, so on Sunday afternoon the stage was set. The copper which stood outside the laundry was filled with water and laced with shaved up soap and "Dad." "Dad" was the washing additive of the day, white tablets sold under the slogan, "Let Dad do it." (I might add, that was the only thing Dad had to do with washing day). Even without "Dad," the washing soap was a fearsome brew, having been concocted from a mixture of mutton fat, caustic soda, resin, Lux and water, mixed at great hazard to life and limb, set in a half kerosene tin cut lengthwise. Later it was cut up and allowed to harden till it took on a wizened and age-worn appearance - it lasted better that way.

Into the copper then went the sheets and towels to soak overnight, while the fire was set with kindling ready for an early start, with larger logs nearby to feed in throughout the day.

Monday morning meant early rising with us kids taking over the breakfast chores while the washing proceeded. The "whites" having boiled were fished out of the copper with the copper stick, an old broom handle, all furry from frequent immersions in boiling water. The scalding, dripping items were manoeuvred into the wicker laundry basked, balanced end on end in an old galvanised tub (we didn't run to a washing trolley), thence into the first rinsing water. From there through the handwringer (preferably operated per courtesy child labour), into the blue rinsing water, coloured through the good offices of Recketts' bag blue, guaranteed to give a whiter wash. Then from the blue water back into the trusty basket and onto the line, long lines propped up with forked sticks. The clothes were fastened down with dolly pegs, which had the added advantage of being able to be used on occasions to dress up as play toys.

Meantime, the clothes with the next degree of soiling went into the copper ready to go through the same procedure till, as the day wore on, into the now soupy copper went the men's most-used work clothes, bearing the marks of sheep dip and drench or whatever was the flavour of the week. The work-socks were my job - they, too, were well laced with the flavour of the week, and often as not matted with grass seeds - as they still were later when it came to darning them.

The last job was to wash the verandahs with the remnants of the hot water, then hosed off with cold. The clothes had to come off the line, be de-grass-seeded if you were unlucky enough to drop them, sorted and folded - but hopefully by now the sun was descending and the air cooling.

And this is where the boiled rice comes in. Is it any wonder that cooking a meal was not by now high on the list of priorities? The evening meal was inevitably cold mutton from the day before's roast, boiled potatoes and "washing day pudding" - boiled rice with milk and sugar.

2002

Of Books and Reading

We grew up as a family of "bookworms." For me, I guess it started with being read to – and I can still remember the day when the words I laboriously picked out for myself came meaningfully together and I was reading - by myself.

I can even tell you when the first wonderful discovery came. I was trying to read a letter on the children's page of *The Queenslander* and suddenly, oh joy! It all made sense.

The Queenslander was an institution for many years – a weekly magazine containing something for all ages – a claim that was attested to by the fact that one of the first sentences of small brother, Ken, was "I bag first look at *The Queenslander,*" that being the chorus from Alan and me when the weekly mail arrived.

We had a bookcase of books – a bookcase of maple (regularly polished with *Shinoleum*) with bevelled glass panels in the doors. It housed a collection of books of varying suitability for children of our ages. I remember giving up on *Anna Karenina;* and the family treasures of volumes of Shakespeare, Wordsworth and Longfellow, beautifully bound, with gold-tipped leaves, were dipped into only occasionally. *The Sentimental Bloke* and other books of bush ballads were more within our capabilities as were Sunday School prizes, *Coles Funny Picture Books* and various annuals handed down by friends. I had favourite adventure stories - *Swiss Family Robinson* with their adventures and resourcefulness when shipwrecked and *Ungava*, set in the Hudson Bay territory of North America, were favourites to be read again and again. I was delighted that *We of the Never Never* was our set book for the scholarship examination and I almost knew it by heart.

One of the real treasures in the bookcase was an eight-volume set of *The Wonder Book of Knowledge*, to which I often had recourse when doing my correspondence lessons - and kept on reading and looking at beautiful pictures far beyond the immediate need, but I did end up with a wide general knowledge.

When we went "bush" to the Tara district, we joined the *Bush Book Club*. I don't know who was responsible for this life-saving scheme for book-hungry bush dwellers. For the princely sum of two shillings and sixpence a year, you could join and receive through the post a parcel of books and magazines, your only responsibility being to forward them on to the next family on the list. We read them, cherished them, mended them where necessary with flour paste and brown paper and sent them on their way. It was an idea I took up again years later when I was responsible for linking up isolated young people when they were past Correspondence Sunday School age.

Occasionally we managed to get a new book. The one which remains in my memory is *The Count of Monte Cristo*. We older ones were anxious to read it (not Dad, as I recall. If it had been about Donald Bradman or Larwood and the bodyline drama, it would have been another story!) So the drill was that as soon as the washing up was finished at night, I made a grab for it and read till my bedtime. Then Alan took over and read till Mother finished the last of the nightly chores in the kitchen, when it was her turn to have it as long as she stayed awake.

With this kind of background, it was hardly my fault if, as I was sometimes accused, I always had my nose in a book.

2008

The Best Thing Since Sliced Bread

Every now and then we hear something described as "the best thing since sliced bread." Frankly, I can't remember what it was that merited this description — but I was set thinking to come up with my version.

First, I thought I might give my vote to what I call "twisties" — those little bits of wire enclosed in plastic that can be used to fasten up packets and plastic bags, to tie up a drooping plant or even, at a pinch, threaded through holes in paper to make impromptu bookbinders.

I carefully hoard those which some butchers use (remember - "Keep a thing; its use will come.") In fact, when it's a matter of deciding which butcher will get my valuable weekly order (two hogget loin chops, half a lamb's fry and a piece of Y-bone steak) the point which can sway my choice is whether he (or she) will use that ghastly contraption that clamps some sticky tape around the plastic bag, or whether he/she fastens it with recyclicable twisties.

Then I thought, "No, useful as twisties are, they can't compare with Velcro, that marvellous modern invention, modelled, I'm sure, on "bindyeyes." It never ceases to amaze me how its little hooks cling to one another, and I gladly accept its replacing press studs, hooks and eyes and even shoe laces. I took some on a trip once. I'd had ideas of using it to fasten up my pockets to hold my passport and money and foil would-be bag snatchers. Of course, once the trip started, I never did get that job done. All that happened was that the Velcro rolled around in my suitcase and fastened to itself and everything else for half the trip, till I found a plastic bag and a twistie and disarmed it.

But eventually I decided that, high as they might be on the list, twisties or Velcro were not the best thing since sliced bread. That honour must go to the day after day convenience of having my morning *Toowoomba Chronicle* delivered safely encased in protective plastic.

To understand the significance of this, we have to go back in history. Once upon a time, something called rain used to fall from the skies and in the morning you would put on your raincoat and gumboots, venture out to the front gate and collect a sodden mass of newspaper pulp. You would take it gingerly inside, drain it on the doormat, then try to open it gently and drape the house with its pages, usually in strips, hoping they would dry enough for you to decipher some news or catch up on the next heart-stopping episode of The Phantom.

But then came the development that we all take for granted, along with TV, pizzas and Big Macs. The Chronicle started arriving rolled and cosily cocooned in a thin film of plastic, and only the heaviest of rain penetrated that.

Admittedly, it now sometimes takes ten minutes to find the end of the plastic and unsheath the momentous news of the day - will it be a headlined picture of Mrs. Brown's escaped cockatoo or a party to celebrate the installation of the one thousandth roundabout? Whatever it is, we can read it, untroubled, clean and dry.

I must say I admire the spirit of the Chronicle decision makers who continue doggedly to have our daily paper plastic wrapped, even though nary a drop of moisture falls from the skies. Either they have great faith that El Nina will relent and we will wake up one morning to the sound of falling rain, or they know from bitter experience that, even in the deepest drought, the very day they omit the wrapping, a passing 5 a.m. scud will leave unclad Chronicles lying wetly on 30,000 (give or take a few) front lawns.

1993

Keep a Thing — Its Use Will Come

"Keep a thing — its use will come" was a motto on which our family was reared (We grew up in the Depression.)

A slight modification was that after seven years you could throw it away, because if its use hadn't come in that time, it was unlikely to. However, my mother had many a heart-rending tale of having allowed herself to be seduced by that modification and thrown some treasure out, only to find the very next day the eventuality arose for which the discarded article would have been ideal. So the Seven-year Rule was honoured more in the breach than in the keeping.

There was one factor that kept the Rule in check. We periodically moved to another location. The magic of the number seven must have had some credence in our household, for it was a belief that Willises never stayed longer than seven years in one place. And since another of my mother's quotes was "Three moves are as good as a fire," we should in the natural course of events have disposed of most of our treasures simply by the passing of time, but even that didn't work out.

It wasn't only in the house that this propensity for saving things ruled. My father and brothers had an insatiable appetite for collecting bits of machinery, old cars and odds and ends that "might come in handy sometime" for mending something else. They even went to the lengths of towing home from time to time some discarded car or engine to add to the treasure trove. Around our sheds would have been heaven to Steptoe and Son.

So with the combined effects of heredity and environment, is it any wonder that my cupboards are full of plastic containers that might come in handy sometime, plastic bags, bottles with lids, bottles without lids, lids without bottles, paper packets, twists off the meatbags and (collector's items these) little bundles of string.

My drawers are full of scrap paper (I might need the backs to scribble on) and my garage of boxes that contained purchases over the last ten years – not to mention magazines and periodicals that I can't bear to throw out. (Even charity booksales don't seem to have much call for 1971 issues of Church News.)

1992

Old bodies from the treasure trove

Ham and Eggs

"Ham and eggs, steak and eggs and a dozen eggs" — that was the standard order of old Pat when he hit town after a long stint in the bush. Not to be wondered at when the local description of the area in which he worked was "A land flowing with milk and honey - a tin of condensed milk for every fourteen blokes and a bee to every 5000 acres."

These reminiscences set me thinking about other eating and drinking orgies indulged in by people coming in touch with delectable delis after a period of deprivation. Two brothers I knew of would meet at the town's Greek cafe (every town had a Greek cafe) and compete at who could drink the most milk shakes, the empties lined up beside them as proof. My brother, a big strong fellow, would line up at the bar with the drinkers and order "a double sas." - sarsaparilla, to the ignorant. He also drove the local dieting ladies crazy with his other indulgence when he visited town - a slab of chocolate and a double ice-cream - and he didn't put on any weight.

My indulgences ranged from a childhood one of 24 aniseed balls. (That cost a penny and they lasted for ages) to an icecream in a cone, to be licked while walking down the main street of Rabaul on infrequent trips to that metropolis. A New Zealand friend's treat when the family visited Rabaul was an apple, divided among the three children. Little Diane's wide-eyed comment one day was, "Mummy says when we go home we'll be able to have a WHOLE apple!"

Take a back seat, ham and eggs!

2002

BETTY WILLIS

What's That You Said?

Once I had as boarders an elderly lady of the old school and a young apprentice cabinet maker. Dennis used to be greatly intrigued by the inherited sayings Ann and I exchanged from time to time.

I'm reminded of this when my friend Beryl and I are working together in the Solomons - and reminded too, how mystifying some of our sayings are to people of a non-English culture.

"Duck your head, Birdie" as a warning of low doorways or beams is a relic of a First World War magazine, picturing an irreverent Aussie soldier in the trenches warning visitor, General Birdwood, of flying shells.

When a period of peace and quiet reigns after a hectic session, "All's quiet on the Western Front" is also a reminder of the First World War. (No, I wasn't there! Mother was a great source of apt sayings.)

"One day nearer victory" as we achieve another step in the task, is a relic of World War Two, while "One more feather and I'd fly" when lacking some necessity to finish a job is from the alleged sayings of an almost featherless cockatoo.

"God bless the Bishop of Aberbrathok" is a useful exclamation when rubbing an itchy back (the product of our friendly fire ants) against a handy post. This comes from mother's story of a Bishop who erected scratching posts during a plague of fleas.

To comment on looking out the window to check on an approaching canoe "It's Alvos with a load of pigs" is a reminder of Beryl's days teaching in a small country school.

When we wonder if doing some washing or working in the

library on a Sunday will offend local custom, Beryl's "If you're going to sin on Sundays, do it behind closed doors," comes in handy. It is another product of her country teaching days when her landlady found her sewing on a button on Sunday with small son watching.

Needing the key from upstairs to gain admission downstairs to the library needs only a call of "Rapunzel, Rapunzel" to bring it hurtling down.

"Go kalap long raun wara" muttered under the breath when someone comes with an unreasonable request, is mine - my Pidgin version of "Go jump in the lake."

The end of a long day brings a run of sayings - "Follow me, Mama," from the one leading the way up the slippery path evokes the memory of a picture in "Punch" of a top-hatted father leading his wife and their brood onto a ship, missing his footstep and disappearing into the water below.

For climbing up the hill with a bell ringing somewhere, Grey's Elegy provides apt sayings - "The curfew tolls the knell of parting day" and "The ploughman homeward plods his weary way."

Back at the house, as one makes a reviving cup of coffee, the other lights a mosquito coil and wanders around waving it and chanting "Hare Krishna, Hare Krishna" hoping no-one is listening and misinterpreting.

I don't know whether it is working in a library with no time to read the books and no light to read at night, but something stimulates me to remember (and at the slightest provocation, quote) reams of poetry from my school days. So suitable occasions will bring forth, in full if necessary, suitable poetic memories.

Need for a decision or action might produce -

> "Which shall it be? Which shall it be?
> I looked at John, John looked at me…"
> or
> "Let us arise and go now, and go to Innisfree"
> or
> "On with the dance, let joy be unconfined. . ."

A passing ship warrants -

> "It was the schooner Hesperus that sailed the wintry sea
> And the captain had taken his little daughter to bear him company..."

A beautiful hibiscus -

> "A thing of beauty is a joy for ever;
> It's loveliness increases; it will never
> Pass into nothingness."

Some unusual activity in the vicinity gives rise to -

> "There was movement on the station
> For the word had passed around
> That the colt from Old Regret had got away…"

though it is lapses of memory, not lack of willingness, that spares Beryl a full rendition of "The man from Snowy River."

2000

Solomon Islands - Guadalcanal-Seghe

When you fly into Henderson Airport at Honiara on Guadalcanal, you look down at places which mark the turning point of the war in the Pacific. Names like Red Beach, Bloody Ridge and Ironbottom Sound are reminders of fierce battles which turned the tide of the Japanese offensive in 1942-43. There are no visible reminders, though, of the Coastwatchers of whom Vice-admiral William Halsey of the United States Navy said - "The coastwatchers saved Guadalcanal, and Guadalcanal saved the Pacific."

But my destination is not Honiara, but Seghe on New Georgia, an hour's flight by small plane to the North West. I clamber in and struggle to fasten the seatbelt but it is hopelessly short.

"Who do you usually carry in this plane - pygmies?" I ask the pilot.

"It's been used in Cambodia," he answers. "The people there are small. Just hang on to the seat in front!"

The two seats in front are occupied by a Gilbertese lady of generous proportions, so I trust in the power of gravity and hang on. There isn't any option, really.

Thankfully there are no airpockets and we have a delightful flight, first along the coast of Guadalcanal, looking on the right-hand side over clear waters of Ironbottom Sound, but can see only a few of the many wartime wrecks which lie there.

On the left-hand side are mountain ranges with forested sides, and strangely forest-free tops often with signs of human habitation, especially tracks winding along the crests of the ridges. I think of the tales our students used to tell of their experiences during their practical years amongst the mountain

65

people, reached after close on two days' walking.

Then it is away from the mainland, and over the world heritage listed Marovo Lagoon with its islands ranging from mountainous forest-covered ones to tiny coral atolls with their fringing reefs and blue-green water and one where flames seem to come from the water itself, a reminder of the fiery activity in the earth below.

We reach the tip of New Georgia and quickly straighten up for Seghe airport. The grass has obviously been cut and we are able to land. The training centre has a contract where the students keep the grass cut. If payment is too slow in coming, there are times when that service is withheld - until the rank growth of grass prevents the planes from landing and the Government is forced to meet its commitment.

This time we land safely and taxi up to the little wooden shed with its "Welcome to Seghe" sign - and I wonder, "Is this still the same airstrip which features in James Michener's "Tales of the South Pacific" - *"Wine for the mess at Seghi."* Certainly these days the planes don't come in bearing supplies for a convivial evening's celebrations!

1998

Of Ablutions and Sundry Related Matters

The tourist brochures of the Pacific picture swaying palms, moonlight on the water, ukeleles and dusky maidens - or handsome men, whichever way your fancy turns. I know a different reality. Apart from the food (How much yam, sweet potato, taro and white rice can the unaccustomed stomach handle?), that reality hinges around ablution and toileting facilities.

Take for example a recent trip. It started uneventfully enough, only the usual glitch with accommodation bookings, saved by being invited by a recently arrived couple to share the transit flat the first night. There my self-esteem took a boost when I discovered they too had taken days of cold showering to work out that the solar heating system did work, once you realised that the hot water came out of the cold water tap.

On to the first village - again, nothing particularly noteworthy. Lovely views through the scantily-curtained doorway of the toilet of both the bay and the path up the hillside were accompanied by the hope that the reciprocal view of approaching villagers wasn't as clear. Ablutions were fairly ordinary - the usual bucket of water and accompanying mug to toss the water over yourself, to be enjoyed in someone's laundry once you had moved five children's clothes out of the way, anchored the skimpy curtain on the window and propped the door shut with a hunk of coral. The galvanised walls were liberally scattered with old nail holes. When what looked suspiciously like a child-height eye blocking a nail hole, a well-aimed mug of water would result in its hasty disappearance.

Next stop - a training centre and luxury - a shower (not working, of course, so back to the bucket and mug), a flushing toilet (as long as you remembered that when the lights went out so did the water) and a large, heavy porcelain handbasin. It seemed a bit shaky, so I handled it gently till the night when I slipped getting out of the shower, put my hand on the basin to steady myself and it fell off the wall. With visions of it crashing to the floor and smashing itself and the water pipes, I struggled to hold it up, but what to do? Yell for help? Hardly fitting in my state of dripping undress. No, at least I must get some clothes on. By the time I had propped the heavy basin up with one hand whilst drying and dressing with the other, I decided there wouldn't be any help within yelling distance anyway, so with much struggling managed to wedge the basin into a bracket on the wall and to my amazement and pride, there it was still holding firmly when I moved on.

The next stop provided a specially constructed edifice for my benefit, a long hike through the sweet potato patch. It had palm leaf walls on three sides, the fourth facing the jungle that hopefully provided privacy, except on the occasions when the men went to cut timber in that direction. At those times, shouted instructions directed them, I presume, to move elsewhere. The shouting was in language, so I didn't know precisely what instructions and reasons were relayed, and thought it politic not to inquire.

The internal furnishing consisted of solid logs surrounding a deep hole in the ground, requiring a delicate balancing act, especially as one hand had to wield a branch vigorously in an endeavour to keep the mosquitoes (more likely than not malaria-carrying anopheles) at bay.

The next place was notable for its "shower." Above a block of concrete an overhead pipe unleashed a breathtaking gush of water - **very** refreshing! Usually it was very skimpily screened and the modest waited till dark to take their ablutions. However, in my honour the lady of the house had erected palm branches and pieces of calico to provide some shelter. The only problem was that as the palm leaves dried they shrank, so it was a race to see which came first - my departure or the disintegration of the palm leaves.

Another move brought another ablution experience. This time a handy husband had provided for his family a shower room with a bench, on which sat buckets of water and where at the appropriate time, another bucket of water appeared from the open fire in the kitchen with the call, "There's hot water for your swim." White coral on the floor, clean but hard on feet accustomed to shoes, even a rope on which to hang your clothes – truly five-star accommodation!

Close by was another palm leaf edifice with, oh luxury, a toilet with a seat. The only problem here was they forgot to warn me of the fire ants, tiny black creatures with a powerful sting that lived up to their name. Their favourite haunt was the toilet bowl, and the "ring of fire" took on a new meaning!

Next stop was a small town, which had grown up around the airport, a rest house, spotlessly clean with a frig, a portagas stove, and a bathroom with a basin and shower and a flushing toilet. I arrived hot and sticky from waiting around dusty airports, rustled up something to eat, luxuriating in the thought of a cool shower, cleaned my teeth, climbed into the shower and turned on the tap - no water! I tried the basin again - this time, no water, I tried all the taps - no water. Back to the kitchen, a cup of water from the frig and with that and the aid of a washer I somehow managed the skimpiest wash of a drought-experienced lifetime.

Next morning when the manageress arrived came the explanation - "I'm sorry, didn't anyone tell you? The town pump gets turned off at nine o'clock at night and there's no water after that."

Do you wonder that my idea of heaven is a clean toilet, long, hot showers and soft white bath towels?

1996

Down the path to the bush toilet

On The Plane – Vanuatu

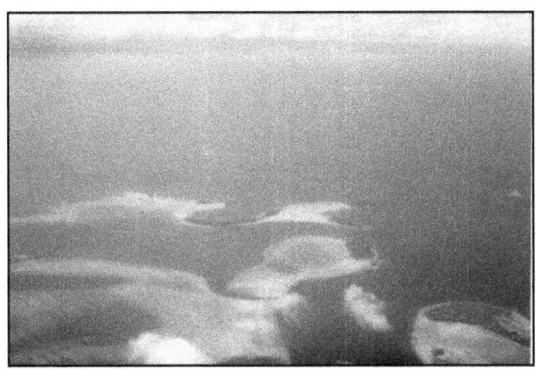

The small plane was flying low, so it was easy to pick out the coral atolls below and to notice that the sea was choppy. One of the passengers commented as we passed over a tidal rip between two islands — "I strong we i strong we i strong" *(he strong where he strong where he strong)* which, being interpreted meant "It's VERY strong."

When the white sandy beaches of a much larger island appeared below, another passenger observed briefly, "Ambrym" - and I remembered that this was the island where my friend, Willi, had been cast ashore with two of his children after a shipwreck.

"I hope the plane is safer," I thought.

In the seat in front of me was a young Ni Vanuatu woman in a nun's habit. I could just see the side of her face, and noticed her lips were moving.

"Saying her daily offices, or praying for a safe trip," I wondered. Then she turned her head to look across to the other side of the plane, and I realised the movement of her lips was due more to Mr. Wrigley than to piety.

1992

No Chance of a Postcard

"Send us a postcard," said Michelle, probably thinking of a touristy Vanuatu with the usual touristy trappings.

"I won't have a chance," I replied.

I didn't think she believed me, so here is why Writers at Work didn't get a postcard from some comfortable hotel under balmy tropic skies.

The tourists were there all right at Brisbane International Airport, 300 or so of them ready for the late-night "Champagne flight." My friend and I must have looked in a slightly different category – five cases or bags each, fingers crossed that the officials would grant us the promised extra weight; wearing the clothes we couldn't fit into our cases – my friend wore four blouses, I wore a cardigan over the top of an all-purpose coat and hoped they wouldn't weigh my handbag, which, with camera, cassette recorder and various anti-this and anti-that medications weighed several kilos. All went well and we embarked – at half an hour after midnight.

Arrived more or less on time; slow through customs with aforesaid 300-odd tourists. Found a taxi-driver who crammed us and our luggage in and set off. Our destination was a backpackers' hostel run by Lucy, a Vanuatu friend who had converted her home after staying in such a hostel in Brisbane.

When we arrived, the place was all in darkness; we knocked and called, called and knocked on different doors – not a sound. The patiently-waiting taxi driver said, "I know where some of the family live; we'll go and see if Lucy and husband are in town." He made an early-morn tour of the town till he found a group of Kava-drinking men and came back to report, "Yes, they should be there."

So back again to knock and call, call and knock, eventually giving up and piling back into the taxi to find an hotel for the night, when lights flooded on and an apologetic and sleepy Lucy and Albert came out – "We had a busy day, went to sleep and didn't wake up."

A few hours' sleep then re-packing to reduce load for local plane; ready in good time for the taxi whose driver had promised to return, but, yes, you've guessed it – no taxi! As check-in drew perilously close, Lucy said, "I'll go out in the streets and try to find a taxi." Anxious waiting again and eventually one of the local minibuses arrived, Lucy having commandeered it in the absence of any taxis. The driver and his offsider loaded us and our luggage aboard and got us to the airport on time.

It was only on our return, five weeks later that we heard the full story, told between shouts of laughter. Lucy had hailed the bus, and said to the passengers, "Yufela go down. Tufela missis laik go long airport." And they all obligingly got down (why they did, in this post-colonial age, I'll never know.) The bus driver assured them he would come back for them. Lucy kept them company; the bus driver did go back, and life went on its casual way.

But you see, Michelle, there **was** no time in Vila to buy and post a card.

1996

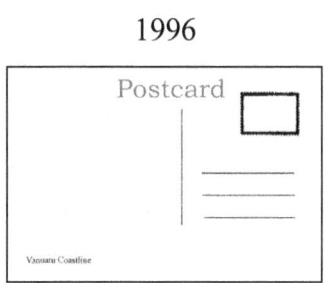

Yupela Laik Save Tok Pidgin?

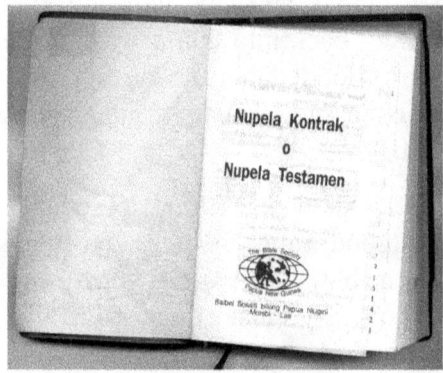

When I first went to Papua New Guinea in 1972, I had to get to work quickly on learning the Pidgin language of that country (officially designated "Neo-Melanesian Pidgin"). It was a trade language developed from simple English, supplemented by expressions from different local languages and from the languages of other Europeans such as German, Portugese and French and other Pacific Islanders whose lives had touched especially the eastern part of the country.

I had to learn on the job because half of my teaching had to be done in that language and the other half in English. It was the only way to cope, since there were 37 language groups represented in the college.

My responsibility was teaching the women, so I battled away with the aid of those who spoke English, and of a comprehensive dictionary of Neo-Melanesian Pidgin compiled by a Father Mihaelic and the recently published Pidgin New Testament. My basic grounding in the language was helped when I started giving special lessons to one of the women who had no-one else in the college who spoke her language. I had access to a very basic series of Pidgin readers, so Waiwali and I worked our way up from sentences such as "Pik i kam" (the pig is coming) and "Pik i kaikai kaukau" (the pig is eating kaukau /sweet potato).

There are variations within a vowel sound, but basically "a" is "ah" or a short sound as in "cab"; "e" is a short sound as in "bet"; "i" is as in "pig" (and also occurs constantly in sentences as a "predicate marker" – "pik i kam" as above); "u" can be a short sound "oo" as in "book"; or long as in "Luke."

The language is strictly phonetic and the hardest thing was to recognise that words were just as they were spelt – once you grasped the basic vowel and consonant sounds.

So "save" as in the title above is the word we use as "savvy." I found Pidgin a fascinating language, with its rich background of sources, and it also produced some hilarious expressions – though I never did discover if it was really true that the Pidgin name for "helicopter" was "mixmaster bilong Jisas Kraist."

I can still remember my sense of achievement when, driving along a road one day I realised I was reading the signs, not spelling them out syllable by syllable. It was akin to my excitement as a child when, before I started school, I realised I was reading in sentences the children's page of a magazine.

In time I became proficient in reading, writing and speaking Pidgin, though I fear the description of another Pidgin-speaking Australian would have applied to me – "He speaks Pidgin like a native – of Australia!" Not all Papua New Guineans became good speakers either. As one local man said to me, "I'm not a good Pidgin speaker. My tongue is too heavy."

Two memorable incidents of Pidgin descriptions remain in my memory. One was when an Australian woman taught a mother with a sickly child to cook scrambled egg. Edna said delightedly to me, "Mi no save bipo dispela pasin long paitim kiau long pok," which being interpreted becomes "I didn't know before this way of beating egg with a fork." ("f" becomes "p" in some local languages.)

The other incident was in Vanuatu where the Pidgin is different, but often the results were comparable. Mary showed me a beanie she had knitted for her baby. It had obviously been made on very fine needles. "Where did you get the needles?" I asked.

Mary replied,

"Mi kasim samting bilong tin fis mo mi kilim witim hama mo mi wokim olsem."

In other words, "I got the keys off fish tins and beat them with a hammer and made them into knitting needles."

Do you wonder that as well as being fascinated with the Pidgin language, I was fascinated with the ingenuity of the women?

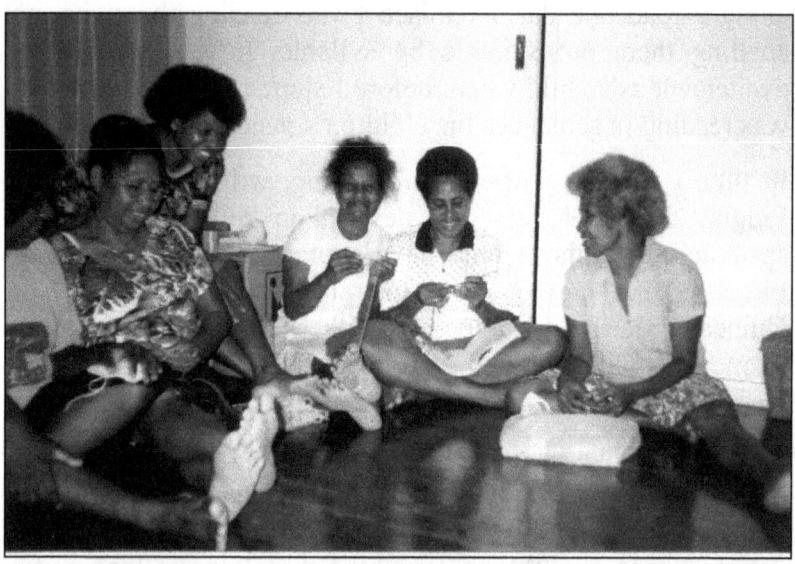

What Am I Here After?

Anyone of my advanced years knows the old joke, "At your age you should be thinking of the hereafter" and the reply, "Yes, I am. Every day I go into a room or stand before a door and say, 'What am I here after.'"

One of my senior lapses recently made me think I should write a treatise on this peculiarity. I bless the microwave every day for its convenience – no porridge saucepan to wash - but it has its limitations. I opened the door the other morning to cook my rolled oats and there was a container of ice cream, except the "ice" no longer applied.

It **was** some comfort when I confessed the incident to a friend to have her reply, "Don't worry. Whenever I want a broom I find myself standing before the refrigerator door asking "What am I here after?"

Another recent aberration of mine was, when walking along a city footpath and hearing footsteps behind me, I checked to see if I should move aside to let a faster walker pass. But I didn't turn around to check, no, I looked up into a non-existent rear vision mirror.

After that, I started to check on some of the other hazards of modern living. The toothpaste tube is one of the most dangerous. A squeeze of lanolin on the brush doesn't have the same cleansing effect as toothpaste, and Deep Heat might be soothing on an aching back, but gives a different reaction in the mouth.

Sprays are another hazard. Fly spray isn't very effective in lubricating a frying pan, and, conversely, cooking spray doesn't seem to worry a wandering blowfly, but it does make a mess of windows. WD40 might be a wonder spray on loosening nuts but not on annihilating mosquitoes nor on cleaning mirrors.

Another recent discovery was that dialling "star, ten, hash" on the cordless phone doesn't activate my hairdryer. This may be because said hair dryer is an old model bought 20 years ago at a garage sale for $5. The remote control for the TV won't operate the automatic garage door – and strangely the reverse also applies.

As for trying to master the mysteries of e-mail after growing up with party telephone lines and mail by horse-drawn buggy – we won't even go there!

2008

Old Age Isn't For Sissies

Who was it said old age isn't for sissies? I've told you before of some of its hazards. Here are some more I've discovered.

One is public signs. I can cope with "men and women," "ladies and gents," and even "sheilas and blokes" when I want to find what is euphemistically known as "the bathroom" or a comfort stop. Sometimes I do have trouble deciding whether that stylised figure is male or female. I really was thrown, though, by the new little man who is supposed to make directions clearer. It wasn't till I found myself outside in the rain that I realised he is running for the exit, not racing to get to the "loo."

I really wonder if a visitor from Outer Mongolia (or even from Mars) finds our sign system easy to interpret.

Medications are another problem. Even if the chemist does deliver them handily done up in clearly labelled packs, you still have to remember to take them, don't you? So, did I take my before breakfast one, and my six after breakfast ones? Have I put my lunch-time one in my handbag if I am going out – or did the phone ring just when I was going to do it? Comes evening – don't forget the before tea one, and the five after tea ones. Oh, and Sunday morning - that's the once-a-week one, taken half an hour before food. Taking it on Sunday is a hangover from missionary days in the tropics, Sunday being the most distinguishable day to remember to take our weekly anti-malarials.

Now, what about my eye-drops? Did I put three lots in last night, or did I fall asleep during the obligatory break in-between. And don't forget the morning ones before I set off for the day.

Remembering where to go is the next problem. When I get to the T-junction at the bottom of our street, I find myself frantically wondering, "Which way do I turn." Right will take me to town, the hospital, the doctor, the dentist or the chiropractor. Left leads to the church, the chiropodist, or the cemetery. Where am I going? Another motorist is tooting madly behind me. Does he want me to get moving or is he trying to tell me my walking stick has fallen off the roof of the car where I put it while I opened the door?

Having remembered where it is I need to go, the next problem is to break into the lines of traffic. This is made hazardous by the fact that half the people who live in South Toowoomba take their children to schools in North Toowoomba, and half the people who live in North Toowoomba take their children to schools in South Toowoomba – and many of them travel in four-wheel drive vehicles, equipped with bull-bars to give them an advantage as they negotiate their way through Toowoomba traffic. What chance does little Mazda 121 have, even if its number plate proclaims it is driven by an Extra Terrestrial Being – that's what ETB signifies, isn't it? Maybe that's why I have such difficulty coping with earthlings and their ways.

2008

www.ingramcontent.com/pod-product-compliance
Lightning Source LLC
Chambersburg PA
CBHW071734040426
42446CB00012B/2358